HORRIBLE HABITATS

Marshes
and Pools

Sharon Katz Cooper

Raintree

www.raintreepublishers.co.uk
Visit our website to find out
more information about
Raintree books.

To order:
☎ Phone +44 (0) 1865 888066
📄 Fax +44 (0) 1865 314091
💻 Visit www.raintreepublishers.co.uk

Raintree is an imprint of Capstone Global Library Limited,
a company incorporated in England and Wales having its
registered office at 7 Pilgrim Street, London, EC4V 6LB
– Registered company number: 6695582

"Raintree" is a registered trademark of Pearson Education
Limited, under licence to Capstone Global Library Limited

Edited by Charlotte Guillain, Rebecca Rissman,
  and Siân Smith
Designed by Joanna Hinton-Malivoire
Picture research by Tracy Cummins and Heather Mauldin
Originated by Chroma Graphics (Overseas) Pte. Ltd
Printed and bound in China by Leo Paper Products

ISBN 978 1 406212 88 4 (hardback)
14 13 12 11 10
10 9 8 7 6 5 4 3 2 1

British Library Cataloguing in Publication Data
Katz Cooper, Sharon.
Marshes and pools. -- (Horrible habitats)
577.6'8-dc22
A full catalogue record for this book is available from the
British Library.

Acknowledgements
The author and publisher are grateful to the following for
permission to reproduce copyright material: Alamy pp. **8**
(© Victor Savushkin), **19**, **20** (© blickwinkel), **24**
(© Peter Arnold, Inc.); Getty Images pp. **5** (© Jerry
Whaley), **6** (© Aldo Sessa); iStockphoto pp. **9**
(© stocksnapper), **28b** (© Nancy Nehring); Minden pp.
10 (© Kim Taylor), **11** (© Stephen Dalton); Nature Picture
Library p. **16** (© Premaphotos); Photolibrary pp. **4**
(© Ron Erwin), **22** (© Chris Mattison); Photo Researchers,
Inc. p. **13** (© Steve Gschmeissner); Photoshot pp. **26**, **27**
(© Bruce Coleman Inc/Joe McDonald); Shutterstock pp. **7**
(© Mike Pluth), **14**, **15** (© Mircea Bezergheanu), **18**
(© Norman Chan), **28a** (© Troy Casswell), **29c**
(© Ed Phillips), **29d** (© BZ Photos); Visuals Unlimited, Inc.
pp. **12** (© Robert Folz), **17** (© Tom Adams), **21** (© David
Sieren), **23** (© GAP Photos LTD/John Glover).

Cover photograph of a frog reproduced with permission of
Getty Images (© Jason Edwards).

Every effort has been made to contact copyright holders
of material reproduced in this book. Any omissions will
be rectified in subsequent printings if notice is given to
the publishers.

Some words are shown in bold, **like this**. You can find
out what they mean by looking in the glossary.

Contents

What is a habitat?

A **habitat** is a place where animals and plants can get the things they need to live. What do they need? Just like you, they need food, water, and shelter.

turtle

Wetlands are **habitats** that are wet at least part of the year. Many plants and animals live where it is warm and wet.

FUN FACT

There are many kinds of wetlands. Swamps, **marshes**, bogs, and pools are all wetlands.

Blood for dinner

Mosquitoes like water. These blood-suckers lay their eggs on the edges of puddles. These eggs hatch into **larvae**, or baby mosquitoes, in one or two days.

mosquito

FUN FACT

Only female mosquitoes actually bite animals to drink blood. Males drink **nectar**. Nectar is a sweet juice that comes from plants.

tube

pupae

larvae

Baby mosquitoes, or **larvae**, live in water. They send up little tubes to breathe. Then they become **pupae**. After a couple of days adult mosquitoes climb out of the pupae skins and fly away.

FUN FACT

Mosquitoes have grooves on their feet that trap air. This helps them walk on water.

11

More blood-suckers!

You will find leeches in some wet **habitats**. A leech is a blood-sucking worm. It attaches to a victim's body with a mouth like a suction cup.

leech

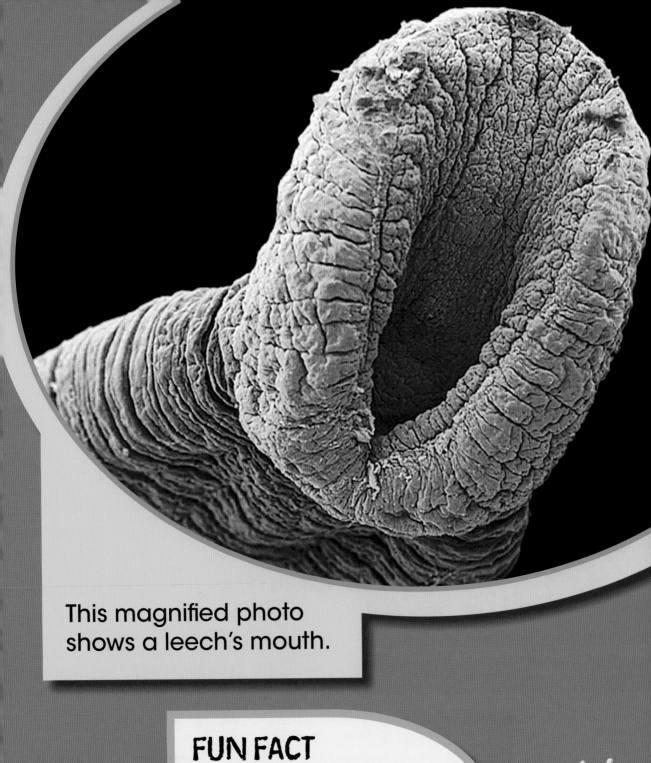

This magnified photo
shows a leech's mouth.

FUN FACT

There are more
than 500 different
types of leech!

13

To pierce an animal's skin some leeches have sharp teeth. Other leeches have a body part that works like a needle. A leech's spit stops blood from forming lumps called **clots**. This means that the leech can suck out the animal's blood until it is full.

FUN FACT

Giant leeches can be almost as long as your arm!

15

flatworm

Wetlands are also home to flatworms. A flatworm shoots a tube out of its underside to pin down its **prey**. Then it shoots **digestive juices** through the tube and sucks up the prey's insides. Digestive juices break food into tiny pieces.

FUN FACT

If the flatworm's food is fresh, the flatworm will turn red as the victim's blood goes up the tube.

Hunting plants

Plants need **nutrients** to stay healthy. Most plants get the nutrients they need from the soil. If the soil has no nutrients, some plants hunt for food instead.

trap

soil

trap

FUN FACT

There are many ways to hunt. Some plants use traps. Others use sticky parts. Still others slurp up their **prey** like a vacuum cleaner!

19

pitcher plant

A pitcher plant is shaped like a vase. Inside, it is slippery. The plant attracts insects with a sweet smell. Once the insects land, they slide down inside the plant. There, **digestive juices** break them apart into food the plant can use.

digestive juices

Gotcha!

A Venus flytrap has rows of tiny hairs on the sides of its leaves. If an insect walks along those hairs, the leaves snap shut. Dinner is served!

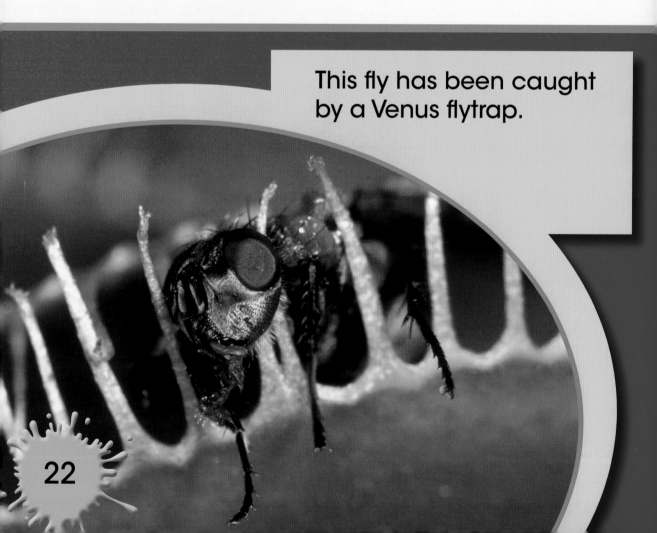

This fly has been caught by a Venus flytrap.

Venus flytrap

23

Strange tails

salamander

The four-toed salamander lives in some **marshes**. It lives in rotting tree roots. When a **predator**, such as a snake, attacks it, the salamander sheds its tail. The tail wriggles like a worm. The rest of the salamander scurries away!

tail

Opossums

Opossums live near some ponds and **marshes**. If a **predator** attacks one, the opossum plays dead. It flops on its side and drips poo from its bottom. If a predator thinks an animal is dead, it sometimes leaves it alone.

dead rabbit

FUN FACT

Opossums eat just about anything. They might eat road-killed animals and dead rats in traps.

Identifying animals and plants

See if you can identify each of these **marsh** or **wetland** plants and animals up close and personal!

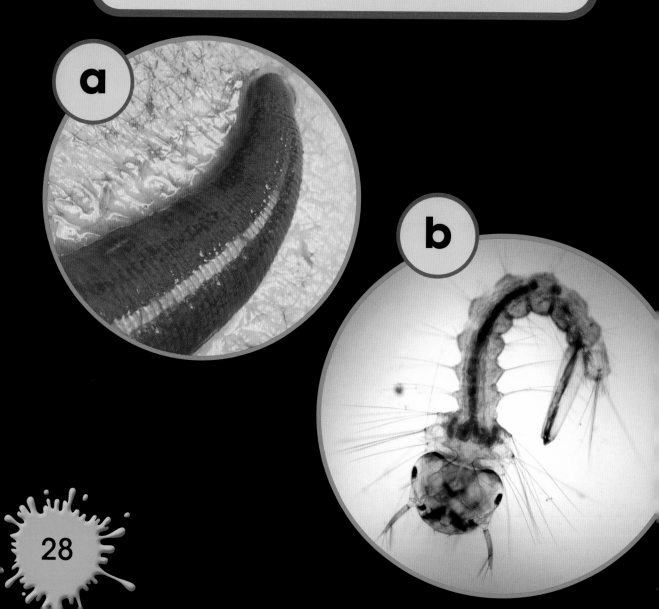

a

b

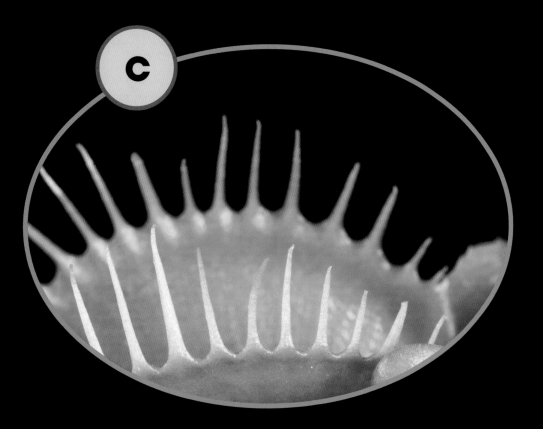

c

d

Glossary

clot lump that forms in liquids such as blood, that stops the liquid from flowing

digestive juices liquids that help break down food into smaller pieces

habitat place where animals or plants live and grow

larvae the young of some types of insect

marsh grassy, wet habitat

nectar sweet juice made by plants

nutrient something animals and plants need to stay healthy and grow

predator animal that hunts and eats other animals

prey animal that is eaten by other animals

pupae before they change into adults some larvae (baby insects) become pupae

wetlands areas that are wet at least part of the year

30

Find out more

Find out

What are leeches closely related to?

Books to read

Bug Books: Mosquito, Jill Bailey (Heinemann Library, 2008)

Wetland Food Chains, Bobbie Kalman, (Crabtree Publishing Company, 2006)

Learning About Life Cycles: The Life Cycle of a Frog, Ruth Thomson (Wayland, 2009)

Websites

http://kids.nationalgeographic.com/Stories/ AnimalsNature/Meat-eating-plants
This website gives you lots of information about meat-eating plants.

http://kids.nationalgeographic.com/Animals/ CreatureFeature/Salamander
Find out some fascinating facts about salamanders on this website.

http://yucky.discovery.com/flash/worm/ pg000219.html
Learn about leeches on this fun website.

Index